DINOSAUR MUMMIES

BEYOND BARE-BONE FOSSILS

DARBY CREEK PUBLISHING

A Division of Oxford Resources, Inc.
Plain City, Ohio

BY KELLY MILNER HALLS
ILLUSTRATIONS BY RICK SPEARS

Like all my books, this effort is dedicated with love to my amazing daughters, Kerry and Vanessa. But I also want to dedicate it to my new pal Stevie, who likes dinosaurs almost as much as she likes soccer. And to Marissa, who hates dogs.

—KMH

Published by Darby Creek Publishing,
a division of Oxford Resources, Inc.
7858 Industrial Parkway
Plain City, OH 43064

Text copyright © 2003 by *Kelly Milner Halls*
Illustrations copyright © 2003 by *Rick Spears*

Design by *Michael Petty*
Petty Productions
www.pettyproductions.com

Cataloging-in-Publication Data

Halls, Kelly Milner, 1957-
Dinosaur mummies : beyond bare-bone fossils / by Kelly Milner Halls;
illustrations by Rick Spears.
1-58196-000-X Hardcover/Library binding
1-58196-034-4 Softcover
p. cm.
Includes bibliographical references and index. – Summary: Learn about
rare dinosaur fossils: the "dinosaur mummies" that are not just bones and
teeth, but also include fossilized soft tissues, like skin, muscle and internal organs and what they can reveal about prehistoric life.
1. Dinosaurs—Juvenile literature. 2. Fossils—Juvenile literature. 3.
Paleontology—Juvenile literature. [1. Dinosaurs. 2. Fossils. 3.
Paleontology.] I. Spears, Rick. II. Title.
QE861.5.H35 2003
567.9—dc21
OCLC: 52256525

Printed in the United States of America

Third printing

4 6 8 10 9 7 5 3

Cover: *Tyrannosaurus rex* Mummy by Rick Spears

ACKNOWLEDGMENTS

This book has evolved almost as continuously as its subjects, thanks to the fascinating ebb and flow of fate. And while some of the changes felt a little uncomfortable at the onset, it's clear now they were shifts that ultimately fit.

With that in mind, let me first thank my daughters, Kerry and Vanessa, for knowing when to leave the office door closed and when to open it to share a reassuring hug. Next, let me thank Tanya Dean, my editor and friend at Darby Creek Publishing for not giving up on these dinosaurs. And thanks to my trio of "Spokane Boys" for rattling my chain and keeping me alive.

Personals aside, let me thank the ranks of remarkable paleontology experts who have been generous beyond measure with their experience, their advice, their encouragement, and their critical expertise. Those people include:

Robert Bakker   *Peter Larson*
Ken Carpenter   *Nate Murphy*
Luis Chiappe   *Dale Russell*
Karen Chin   *Paul Sereno*
Cristiano Dal Sasso   *Rick Spears*
Kristin Donnen   *Mark Thompson*
David Gillette   *Colleen Whitney*
Thomas Holtz

—KMH

CONTENTS

INTRODUCTION

Living my kid years in Friendswood, Texas, was like growing up in Reptile Acres. With steel-toed boots on my feet and the *Golden Book Guide to Reptiles and Amphibians* in my back pocket, I caught—and released—every safe species in the woods. That's what the field guide was for: to help me know what I was getting ready to grab! Snakebites or nasty lizard nips could ruin a perfectly good day.

Snakes, toads, frogs, salamanders, skinks, lizards. You name the cold-blooded critter, and I got up-close and friendly with it. But my favorite childhood memories revolve around the American **anole**. Those color-changing lizards scampered up every warm brick wall in our cul-de-sac. And if I could have shape-shifted, I would have shimmied up with them.

Their twitching, throbbing tails broke off to help them escape capture. Then, like a miracle of science fiction, within a few weeks the tail would start to grow back. That was so cool! But watching their leathery, jelly-bean-sized eggs hatch into miniature, survival-ready anoles was mouth-dropping awesome. Even a dead specimen captured my imagination. Nothing fascinated me more than finding a sun-bleached skeleton or the dried-out mummified body of a dead adult lizard.

Within a few weeks the tail will grow back on this American anole.

4

FROM LIZARD LOVE TO DINOSAUR DIGS

Those kid years came rushing back when I made my first trip to a natural history museum. I stood speechless (pretty amazing for a talk-a-mile-a-minute girl) when I looked up at dinosaur skeletons mounted in life-like positions right in front of me. They weren't exactly like my lizard buddies, but they were freakishly close. And they were *huge*, especially compared to my five-inch-long anoles. From that moment, I was hooked on **paleontology**, the study of dinosaurs and dinosaur times. For many years to come I dreamed of digging for and discovering those amazing bones.

My dream came true when I grew up and became a writer. I got lots of chances to dig dinosaur bones with paleo-experts. And I still love to write about these mysteries from the past. Almost every dinosaur fossil discovery was similar to a lizard memory I had. But until I heard about a special fossil named Leonardo, I had never realized that dead dinosaur bodies could dry out and become mummified, too—kind of like the withered, dry anole corpses I had seen in Texas. I thought the only dinosaur fossils on earth were bones or teeth—you know, the *hard* stuff.

I was so excited about dinosaur mummies that I just had to write a whole book about them! Dinosaur skeletons and dinosaur mummies—two kinds of fossils that show us a world and time we can only find in our imaginations. Bones are terrific fossils, because they tell us a lot about how dinosaurs died. But dried up, fossilized skin, hearts, muscles, and goop-filled stomachs tell us some surprising things about how they lived.

The first step of our search for dinosaur mummies is to find out just how those dinosaurs were so well-preserved for so long.

Author Kelly Milner Halls and illustrator Rick Spears help out at a dinosaur fossil dig site in Montana.

Photo © Jeff Miller

DIGGING UP THE DIRT ON FOSSILS

W<small>E SEEM TO BE BORN WITH</small> fossil fascination. We dig in our backyards hoping to find a fossil. Any rock or bit of hard material is examined closely for strange impressions—"fossil marks." Of course, most of our finds are not really fossils, just curious-looking rocks that stir our imaginations.

But what *is* a fossil? According to dinosaur scientist Dr. Luis Chiappe of the Natural History Museum of Los Angeles County in California, a **fossil** is any trace of an ancient organism. An **organism** is any living thing—plant or animal. Most fossils are actually a plant or animal's remains (or impressions of their remains) that have turned to stone. Fossils help us to "see" the past.

Lizard skeleton impression fossil

THE MOST COMMON FOSSILS: BONES

Scientists are beginning to understand the process that turned once-living creatures into stone-cold fossils. After an animal died, its body gradually was covered with layer after layer of fine soil. Sometimes the soil covered the dinosaur corpse before its soft tissue—skin, muscles, and internal organs—had decayed completely. Then those meaty parts continued to decay under the soil. As the soft tissue vanished, the soil resettled against the bare bones and teeth—the hard materials.

Poplus oak leaf impression fossil

Fossilized bones in rock

6

The fossilization process worked in stages. The hard parts were **porous**, able to absorb things like a sponge. First, minerals filled the **pores**, or small holes in the bones. Over time, if they absorbed the right minerals through the dirt, those bones and teeth became fossils. As the actual bones decomposed, the minerals filled the spaces where actual bones had been, duplicating the bone itself. All of the original bone disappeared, but in its place was a fossil, an exact copy of the bone, made of mineralized rock. Finally, layers of dirt and rock formed over those prehistoric copies. The fossils lay buried for what scientists believe to be millions of years.

Over time, the weight of those soil and rock layers crushed some of the fossils, but the same soil and rocks protected others. Then, from time to time, the earth rumbled and changed because of volcanic eruptions, earthquakes, and the shifting of subcontinental sheets of rock, called **tectonic plates**. The layers were

Dirt and rock material must be removed carefully to expose fossils.

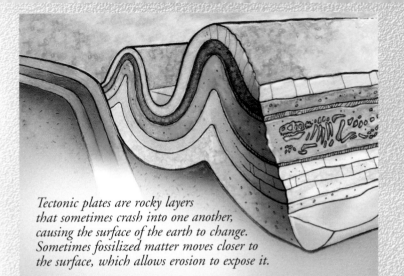

Tectonic plates are rocky layers that sometimes crash into one another, causing the surface of the earth to change. Sometimes fossilized matter moves closer to the surface, which allows erosion to expose it.

Tectonic Plates:
How the Earth Rocks and Rolls

Scientists—geologists and paleontologists—explain that dinosaurs were buried several million years ago under layer after layer after layer of dirt and rock.

These layers are at least a mile thick, according to Denver Museum of Natural History paleontologist Ken Carpenter. So how did the prehistoric remains rise to the surface to be discovered by fossil hunters?

To answer that question, you have to understand a little about Earth's geology. Within the earth are underground slabs of moving stone called **tectonic plates**. The constant motion of these plates just beneath the Earth's crust creates cracks and moves the rock layers. Some layers can sink. But other layers, rich in dinosaur fossils, are pushed toward the surface.

How do we know the plates are moving? An earthquake is a sign of tectonic shifts. Even volcanic activity can be a sign of tectonic motion. When a volcano erupts, the layers of rock go up, while other layers slip down.

The earth's surface changes when the plates bump against each other. Sometimes the changes are so tiny you can't see them—maybe the crack in your sidewalk gets a fraction of an inch wider. Sometimes the energy of the collision is so great, it's impossible to miss, like the famous Northridge, California, earthquake of 1994, which caused more than 15 billion dollars' worth of property damage. And sometimes something amazing happens: Dinosaurs are "reborn"—as fossils.

shaken up, shifting the remains of the prehistoric creatures back to the top of the heap. Once they resurfaced, wind and rain caused natural **erosion**, which gently broke down the softer dirt and rock that had protected the fossils. Tiny cracks in the rock filled with water. Once winter set in, the water froze and expanded, making the cracks in the stones bigger. Then, when spring arrived, the rain and wind loosened this protective rock.

Erosion continued, stripping away enough of the last layers to expose the fossilized bone. It was only a matter of time before eagle-eyed explorers found the fossilized dinosaur bones and shared them with the rest of the modern world. Those became (and will continue to become) the prehistoric fossil treasures you can see in natural history museums today.

Earth's Rarest Fossils: Dinosaur Mummies

Human mummies are not fossils. They are made of soft tissue that has been preserved by special tars, salts, wrappings, or climate.

Kenneth Garrett / National Geographic Image Collection

Bones and teeth are great for building skeletons and for showing a dinosaur's internal bone structure, but what about a dinosaur's *outsides?* What did its skin, muscles, and fleshy parts look like? Make way for the dinosaur mummies!

The term "mummy" is fun, but it is only partly correct when it comes to dinosaurs. "Mummification" means something different among paleontologists than it does among **archaeologists**. Archaeologists study the remains of past human life and ancient cultures. Mummies of animals and human beings, like ancient Egyptian mummies, were preserved on purpose using special tars, salts, and wrappings. Mummies in South America were naturally preserved by the sub-zero temperatures of the high-mountain winters. Those mummies were not mineralized. Their skin, hair, and internal organs are still human tissue.

Very rarely, nature saved bits and pieces of a dinosaur's soft tissue along with bone. Dinosaur mummies don't have soft tissue left intact like human mummies.

8

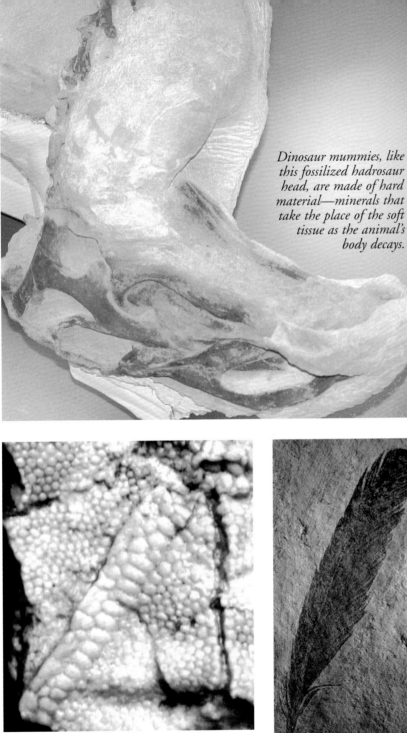

Dinosaur mummies, like this fossilized hadrosaur head, are made of hard material—minerals that take the place of the soft tissue as the animal's body decays.

Left: Fossilized skin of an unhatched dinosaur
Right: Impression of a feather

Instead, they're *fossilized* mummies—made of stone. Scientists haven't solved the mystery of the fossilized dinosaur mummies yet. They think that in some special instances, dinosaur skin turned to leather before the dead animal was buried or had decomposed. After it was covered by muddy or sandy water, the process of decay was very slow. As a result, dinosaur skin, muscle, and internal organs had time to absorb and be surrounded by minerals, like calcium carbonates, before the soft tissue rotted away.

The absorbed minerals made a way for the soft tissue to be fossilized, like the hard material. Some are rock copies that look like the animal looked when it died. Other fossilized mummies are found as bits and pieces, usually skin or feather impressions, saved as negative images, like your footprint in soft, wet sand.

Dinosaur mummies are rare. They help us learn more about how dinosaurs lived, just as fossilized bones reveal some of the secrets of how they died. Together, these ancient puzzle pieces tell us an amazing story of our planet's prehistoric past.

First-Time Find: The Sternberg Mummies

FOR CENTURIES, WE HAVE STUDIED everything from weather patterns to stars that gleam light years from our world. It might seem that we've been discovering the secrets of fossilized dinosaurs for a long time, too. But paleontology, the study of prehistoric life, is a fairly new science.

French scientist Baron Georges Cuvier first claimed in 1777 that fossilized ocean-bound reptiles' bones were the remains of **extinct** animals. The word "**dinosaur**" came even later—64 years later. In 1841, British anatomist Sir Richard Owen invented the word "dinosauria," which means "terrible reptile."

By the 1870s, dinosaur mania had begun. In the United States, "Bone War" rivals Edward Drinker Cope and Othniel Charles Marsh began their famous "who-can-find-more-dinosaurs?" competition in 1877. Kansas's fossil digger, Charles H. Sternberg, was a leader in their army of experts. During the years that he worked with Cope and Marsh (separately), he discovered dozens of important bone beds.

Then in 1908, Charles Sternberg's son George stumbled upon a discovery that would forever change the way paleontologists saw dinosaurs. On a wind-whipped sandstone ridge in Wyoming, George unearthed fossilized dinosaur skin. It belonged to a species that became known as *Edmontosaurus*. Until that time, fossils were remnants of hard materials: bones and teeth.

Top: Baron Georges Cuvier
Middle: Edward Drinker Cope
Bottom: Othniel Charles Marsh

In her book *The Sternberg Fossil Hunters, A Dinosaur Dynasty*, the late Katherine Rogers quotes from George's journal: *Imagine the feeling that crept over me when I realized that here for the first time, a skeleton of a dinosaur had been discovered wrapped in its own skin. That was a sleepless night for me.*
—George Sternberg, 1908

Today experts at the Sternberg Museum of Natural History in Fort Hays, Kansas, say that the *Edmontosaurus* specimen "was the first dinosaur found covered in fossilized flesh." Henry F. Osborn, curator of New York City's American Museum of Natural History, bought the remarkable fossil specimen. Still proudly exhibited in a glass case today, the Sternbergs' first "dinosaur mummy" was made of mineralized stone—not dehydrated flesh like human mummies that have been found preserved in Egypt, China, and South America.

Two years after George found his historic *Edmontosaurus*, his brother Charlie found a second *Edmontosaurus* mummy. "The dinosaur died in quicksand," wrote their father Charles in his autobiography, *Hunting Dinosaurs in the Bad Lands of the Red Deer River*, "which helped to preserve its contorted death pose as it fought to escape." According to Sternberg, the speed of the dinosaur's burial "allowed much of the skin, especially on the chest and legs, to be preserved in an inflated, lifelike position."

Charlie's mummy was sold to the Senckenberg Museum in Frankfurt, Germany, where it remains to this day. "It's displayed in a cool way," says Black Hills Institute paleontologist Peter Larson, who is an expert in **casting**—making copies of dinosaur mummies—and who excavated the Chicago Field Museum's prized *Tyrannosaurus rex*, Sue. "There is a balcony with a hole cut through the floor, so you can view the mummy directly underneath you. Then, if you find your way to his floor, you discover his tomb, a glass case, so you can see him from every angle. Nobody speaks aloud in that darkly lit room," Larson says. "It feels almost sacred."

Two views of the first dinosaur mummy ever discovered: the Sternberg Edmontosaurus. *Fossilized flesh is attached to the bones.*

What Is an *Edmontosaurus*?

Edmontosaurus was one of the biggest **hadrosaurs**, or duckbill dinosaurs, that has ever been discovered. It was named for the Canadian region where it was found: Edmonton. Fossil remains tell us that the adult of this species was between 33 and 42 feet long, from duckbill to tail. Thousands of them thrived 65 to 73 million years ago during the **Cretaceous Period** of the **Mesozoic Era**.

This herbivorous—plant-eating—dinosaur walked on two stocky legs with three-toed feet. It used its mitten-handed forelegs only occasionally. *Edmontosaurus* had a toothless beak, similar to the beaks of modern-day birds, but not as pointed. Inside its mouth grew hundreds of grinding teeth, perfect for eating conifer needles, seeds, and other plant life.

Edmontosaurus was probably a herding, **migratory** animal that followed the rainy patterns of its tropical prehistoric world—a world that probably looked something like the thick, green, coastal regions of modern New Orleans. No one knows exactly how *Edmontosaurus* or any other dinosaur went extinct, but hadrosaurs lived in healthy groups for thousands of years.

You may want to see those dinosaurs for yourself. Here are the three great museums where the Sternbergs' dinosaur mummies now sleep:

American Museum of Natural History
Central Park West at 79th Street, New York, NY 10024
http://www.amnh.org

Sternberg Museum of Natural History
3000 Sternberg Dr., Hays, Kansas 67601
http://www.fhsu.edu/sternberg/

Senckenberg Nature Museum
Senckenberganlage 25, D-60325, Frankfurt, Germany
http://www.senckenberg.uni-frankfurt.de/dino/dino03.htm

Edmontonosaurus *(death pose)*
33 to 42 feet long
Canada
Herbivore
Cretaceous Period
Mesozoic Era

Considered one of the most important dinosaur discoveries ever unearthed, the second mummy revealed a duck-like skull that earned hadrosaur-type dinosaurs like *Edmontosaurus* the nickname of "duckbills." Its stomach contents had also been preserved. The pine, or **conifer**, needles and seeds convinced paleontologists that duckbills were land-bound dinosaurs, rather than aquatic, as they had previously believed.

In 1913 the Sternberg family found and excavated a third duckbill with fossilized skin in Alberta, Canada. It was sold to the British Museum of Natural History, but on its voyage by ship across the Atlantic, the ship and all of its cargo, including this historic dinosaur discovery, sank to the bottom of the ocean. They never saw the attack coming.

"Torpedoed by a German secret raider," says world-famous paleontologist and head of the Jurassic Park Institute, Dr. Robert T. Bakker. "Tragic."

Even so, the Sternbergs' dinosaur mummy legacy lives on, both here in the United States and in Germany.

Who Were the Sternbergs?

Charles H. Sternberg was born in New York State in 1850. During his career as a freelance fossil hunter, which began when he was only 17 years old, Charles worked with and for some of the most famous dinosaur collectors in history. These included Edwin Drinker Cope and Othniel Charles Marsh, America's famous "Bone War" rivals. He later experienced his own fossil competition with the American Museum of Natural History's famous paleontologist, Barnum Brown.

Sternberg's three sons, George (1883-1969), Charlie (1885-1981), and Levi (1894-1976) followed in their father's dinosaur-hunting footsteps. Together, the four Sternbergs made up one of history's most interesting fossil-hunting families.

American Museum of Natural History

Charles Sternberg with his discovery of a dinosaur mummy in Edmonton, Canada.

13

Scipionyx: Italy's Baby Dinosaur has Guts

When Dr. Cristiano Dal Sasso started his studies at the University of Milan in the late 1980s, Italy had no dinosaurs of its own. But Dr. Dal Sasso loved fossils—what he calls "witnesses to life history"—and had been fascinated with them since he was a small boy. He dreamed of finding fossils of Italian dinosaurs, ones that would put his homeland on the paleo-map. In the meantime, he studied the fossils from prehistoric oceans—ferocious whale-like reptiles called **mosasaurs** that had rows of dagger-like teeth, sharks, sea turtles, shellfish, and more—in order to learn his trade.

Scipionyx
Benevento Province, Italy
Carnivore
Cretaceous Period
Mesozoic Era

14

Dinosaurs by Land, Marine Reptiles by Sea

Dinosaurs ruled the land during Earth's Mesozoic Era, from its **Triassic Period** (245-208 million years ago) to its **Jurassic Period** (208-146 million years ago) and through to the end of the Cretaceous Period, 65 million years ago. But what ruled the Mesozoic marine regions—its oceans, bays, and seas?

Fish and shellfish populated the waters, of course. But paleontologists call the large creatures that ruled the waters **marine reptiles**—not water dinosaurs. Why are they not considered dinosaurs?

The word *dinosaur* means "terrible lizard." Lizards are reptiles that live only on land, not in large bodies of water. But in the Mesozoic Era, dozens of other kinds of reptiles did live in the water, thus the name marine reptiles. And paleontologists study them, too.

Does the same thinking apply to prehistoric animals that flew through the air? Absolutely. It may be tempting to call pterosaurs "flying dinosaurs," but the correct phrase is "flying reptiles."

Paleontologists keep dinosaurs on solid ground—where they belong.

Fossilized skeleton with soft tissue (claws, muscle, windpipe, liver, and intestine) of Ciro, Italy's baby Scipionyx.

Earlier, in 1980, an amateur bone digger named Giovanni Todesco had made a discovery in the Benevento Province near Naples, Italy, that no one knew about. In a rock formation known for prehistoric marine or ocean fossils, Todesco found a twisted, finely detailed skeleton in a flat slab of limestone. He thought it might be the fossil of a reptile or a bird, so he just packed up the mysterious fossil and put it away.

When the film *Jurassic Park* came to Italy, Todesco remembered his forgotten fossil. He took the specimen out of storage and showed it to Dr. Giorgio Teruzzi, Curator of Paleontology at the Museum of Milan where Dr. Dal Sasso worked. Soon, the experts confirmed that the fossil was the skeleton of a very young dinosaur, one that had lived 113 million years ago. Thirteen years after its discovery, Todesco's fossil finally made Dr. Dal Sasso's dreams come true. Italy had its very first dinosaur fossil!

From 1994 to 1997, Dr. Dal Sasso carefully prepared the ten-inch-long *Scipionyx* fossil, nicknamed Ciro. Almost immediately, Dr. Dal Sasso realized some of Ciro's soft tissue had been preserved along with the skeleton. "We used very small chisels and needles rather than acids to remove the limestone from the fossilized bones," he says, "to avoid damaging any of the organic remains."

Which bits of flesh had been turned to stone? Several different parts lay fossilized before him: **horny sheaths**, claws on its fingers; muscle tissue at the chest and near the tail section; the windpipe; traces of the liver; and the entire intestine—the little dinosaur's gut.

"All of the above-mentioned soft parts, except the intestine and the supposed liver, are 3-D mineralized tissues, and not simply imprints," Dr. Dal Sasso explains. "The intestine is actually an **endocast**, as shown by the folds of the inner layers of the gut."

© Museo di Storia Naturale di Milano and Fabio Fogliazza

A 3-D model of young Ciro as he may have looked.

Baby Bathed in Blue

When *Scipionyx* was available for other scientists to study, a team from Oregon State University and the College of Charleston in South Carolina examined Ciro under **ultraviolet light**. "Ultraviolet light does a peculiar thing to certain kinds of organic tissue," says South Carolina paleontologist Willem Hillenius. By "**organic**," Hillenius means something left behind by a once-living organism. Fossilized bone turns bright orange; fossilized soft tissue or flesh turns fluorescent blue.

Ciro, or "Skippy" to some American scientists, was bathed in blue. Here was a wonderful dinosaur mummy specimen. "We found a nicely preserved colon and large intestine," says Oregon scientist Nicholas Geist. "And the liver area seemed to absorb the light," meaning it was there, but harder to analyze.

Hillenius believed that the location of Ciro's liver meant he was crocodilian and cold-blooded, like modern-day reptiles. That means he would have had to absorb heat from his environment, because he was unable to generate heat of his own. Dr. Dal Sasso does not agree, however. He believes the rest of *Scipionyx*'s bird-like anatomy means he had the same "warm-blooded-like metabolism" found in most small **theropods** (two-legged meateaters)—a metabolism more like that of modern birds.

Ciro (or Skippy) is a remarkable fossil that will tell us more about the inner world of dinosaurs as technology improves in the years to come.

Ciro under a black light.

Willem J. Hillenius

Who Is Dr. Cristiano Dal Sasso?

Cristiano Dal Sasso was born in Italy on December 9, 1965. "Since I was a child, I have been fascinated by fossils," he says. "Not only paleontology, but all natural sciences caught my interest."

Before *Scipionyx* was discovered in Italy, Dr. Dal Sasso studied ancient marine reptiles—large, water-bound animals that thrived in a prehistoric sea. He found, studied, and named two new marine species. But *Scipionyx* was his dream-come-true. "A truly magnificent fossil," he says.

While he was studying *Scipionyx*, Dr. Dal Sasso had a very serious car accident and lost his right leg. After he recovered from the injuries, the dedicated scientist continued his important work. Dr. Dal Sasso has gone on to study two new Italian dinosaur finds: saltriosaur, a large meat-eater similar to *Tyrannosaurus rex*, and an unidentified duckbill dinosaur. He is also studying Italian dinosaur tracks and has written a book about his country's dinosaur history.

© Museo di Storia Naturale di Milano

Dr. Cristiano Dal Sasso holding Italy's first dinosaur, Ciro the Scipionyx.

By studying the fossil clues, Dr. Dal Sasso has discovered some important facts about Ciro, the only *Scipionyx* specimen that has ever been discovered. "Incomplete formation of the tiny bones and no first teeth replacement (Ciro still had its baby teeth) suggest the specimen was no more than two weeks old when it died," he says. The fact that its intestine was short means the tiny meat-eater was able to absorb food nutrients quickly. Although its feet were missing, the rest of the fossil anatomy tells Dr. Dal Sasso that Ciro probably had feet with "three toes," he says, "but no *Velociraptor*-like specialized claw."

According to Dr. Dal Sasso, Ciro probably died when a storm raged and swept him into a nearby lagoon. That lagoon quickly covered and preserved his tiny body so it could fossilize and keep him safe until he was discovered in 1980. The real hatchling is gone, but paleontologists at his new home, the Museo Civico di Storia Naturale in Milan, will make sure Ciro, the very first Italian dinosaur, will never be forgotten.

17

WILLO: A THESCELOSAURUS WITH HEART

The remains of Willo, a Thescelosaurus. Its fossilized heart can be seen in the center.

© North Carolina Museum of Natural Sciences

WHAT SECRETS BEAT WITHIN the heart of a dinosaur? North Carolina paleontologist Dr. Dale Russell knows, because he has captured—and has been captured by—the heart of Willo.

Who is Willo? She is a 13-foot-long, 66-million-year-old *Thescelosaurus* fossil on display at the North Carolina Museum of Natural History in Raleigh. Willo's mineralized heart has paleontologists wondering if some dinosaurs might have been warm-blooded, and therefore able to generate their own body heat.

Oregon dinosaur investigator Mike Hammer and his son Jeff found "the little dinosaur with heart" in South Dakota's Hell Creek Formation in 1993. The Hammer family had searched frequently for fossils on their travels. This discovery seemed special from the start, though, because of a strange fossilized mass they noticed in the animal's chest cavity. Hammer asked his friend, family practitioner and amateur paleontologist Dr. Andrew Kuzmitz, to run a few tests. A reconstructed 3-D CT scan at Ashland Community Hospital in Oregon revealed Willo's iron-rich, grapefruit-sized, four-chambered heart.

Hot or Cold?

What is the main difference between warm-blooded and cold-blooded animals? Warm-blooded animals have the ability to regulate their body temperature internally, while cold-blooded animals depend on their environments to keep warm enough or cool enough to survive.

Lizards, alligators, and other cold-blooded animals bask in the warmth of the sun to raise their body temperatures, and they dig into sand or swim in cool water to lower their internal thermometers.

Warm-blooded animals can generate their own heat by becoming more active. Humans and some other mammals, like horses, can cool down by perspiring. When you run, you probably feel warmer, then start to sweat, and finally feel your heart beating stronger and faster. This means your warm-blooded heart is doing its job. Dr. Dale Russell believes Willo's heart worked like yours, too.

The alligator is a cold-blooded animal.

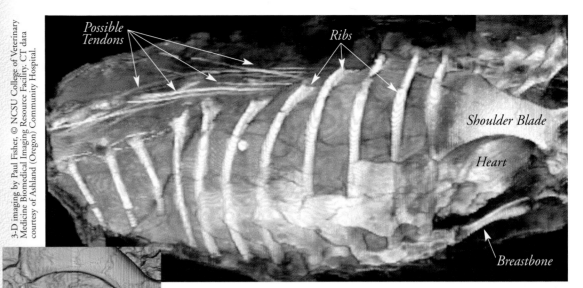

3-D imaging by Paul Fisher, © NCSU College of Veterinary Medicine Biomedical Imaging Resource Facility. CT data courtesy of Ashland (Oregon) Community Hospital.

Possible Tendons

Ribs

Shoulder Blade

Heart

Breastbone

An image of a CT scan of Willo's remains with key parts labeled.

A colorized 3-D CT scan of Willo's grapefruit-sized, four-chambered heart.

Three years later, Hammer sold Willo to the North Carolina museum. Soft tissue fossilization was so uncommon that Dr. Russell had a second CT scan done, just to confirm Dr. Kuzmitz's original findings. The results gave Dr. Russell a reason to smile—and to propose some important new dinosaur theories.

"Willo's heart tells us that all or most dinosaurs probably had higher-than-reptilian metabolic rates," says Dr. Russell, though not all experts agree. If he's right, then dinosaurs were more physically active than cold-blooded reptiles, such as crocodiles and alligators.

But crocodiles and alligators have four-chambered hearts, too. So what makes Willo different? The CT scan showed that, like mammals, only one massive blood vessel controlled Willo's blood flow. In contrast, two aortas pump within the four-chambered hearts of cold-blooded reptiles. "Willo's heart has a single systemic aorta," Russell says, "rather than the double aorta found in crocodilians." This fact supports his theory of warm-blooded dinosaurs.

Who Is Dr. Dale Russell?

Dale Russell's love for fossils began in elementary school. His older brother handed him a **trilobite** and pieces of a mammoth's tooth. A trilobite is an ancient ocean creature. Dr. Russell earned his master's degree in paleontology at the University of California at Berkeley and his Ph.D. in geology at Columbia University. In 1971, he introduced a new idea that an asteroid might have crashed through the earth's atmosphere from space, slamming into the earth. That impact and its after-effects —tidal waves, dust clouds, climate changes—might have pushed the dinosaurs toward extinction.

Dr. Russell has collected dinosaur fossils in North America, South America, Europe, Africa, and Asia. Today, he is the senior curator of paleontology at the North Carolina Museum of Sciences. He also directs the Center for the Exploration of the Dinosaurian World, an organization dedicated to making more dinosaur discoveries.

N.C. Museum of Natural Sciences

Dr. Dale Russell beside his famous dinosaur mummy, Willo.

A four-chambered heart isn't the only thing that makes Willo special, though. She was also the first *Thescelosaurus* ever found that had a completely intact skull. In addition, other soft tissue was fossilized along with the heart. Willo had fossilized tendons still attached to her spine and fossilized cartilage still clinging to her ribs. According to Dr. Russell, other shadows and shapes revealed in the CT scans suggest Willo may have other organs preserved, too.

How is this rare fossilization possible? Willo must have died at the right time and in the right place—in waterlogged, oxygen-free sand. A process called **saponification** may have set in. Saponification changes soft tissue into a soap-like substance that slows natural decay long enough for the shape and structure of the heart to be duplicated in fossil form.

"Willo was rapidly covered by fine sand in poorly oxygenated swamp water," Dr. Russell says. Her body was protected from scavengers while iron carbonates seeped into the heart's soft tissue to form a fossilized copy.

Is this *Thescelosaurus* the find of a lifetime?

"Absolutely," says Dr. Russell. He hopes the technology that opened Willo's heart to the world will encourage new discoveries. "I hope and anticipate more hearts will be found. From now on, we will definitely be looking."

Thescelosaurus
Hell Creek Formation,
South Dakota Herbivore
Cretaceous Period
Mesozoic Era

Is Willo *Really* a Girl?

Well, there is a 50-50 chance! Not enough evidence exists to tell us if Willo the *Thescelosaurus* was a boy or a girl—so we may never know. Fossil hunter Michael Hammer named his fossil "Willo" after the wife of the rancher who gave him permission to search his land for prehistoric bones. Some host families like to feel that they are part of the fossil-finding team, so the discoveries are often "named" in their honor. It's a fun way to thank them for their support. Willo became a "she"—all in the name of fossil friendship!

SINOSAUROPTERYX: A FEATHERED FIND IN CHINA

CHINA HAS BEEN A DINOSAUR DIGGER'S DREAM for more than 100 years. Adventurers like Roy Chapman Andrews scoured the Chinese countryside, finding scores of fossilized bones. So it wasn't all that surprising when farmer Li Yin Fang found the first *Sinosauropteryx* fossil in his home province of Liaoning in 1994.

For decades, Liaoning locals had unearthed all kinds of other fossils: leaves, insects, fishes, frogs, and more. But the tiny meat-eater that had been preserved for about 120 million years was something remarkable. According to Dr. Mark Norell of the American Museum of Natural History, the first U.S. paleontologist allowed to examine the fossil, this turkey-sized dinosaur once may have been covered in feathery down.

For several years, paleontologists like Dr. Norell, Dr. Robert Bakker, and Dr. Luis Chiappe have wondered if dinosaurs might be related to modern-day birds. These two animal types have some very interesting skeletal similarities. Fossils show that some dinosaurs could have been covered

Sinosauropteryx
Liaoning, China
Carnivore
Early Cretaceous Period
Mesozoic Era

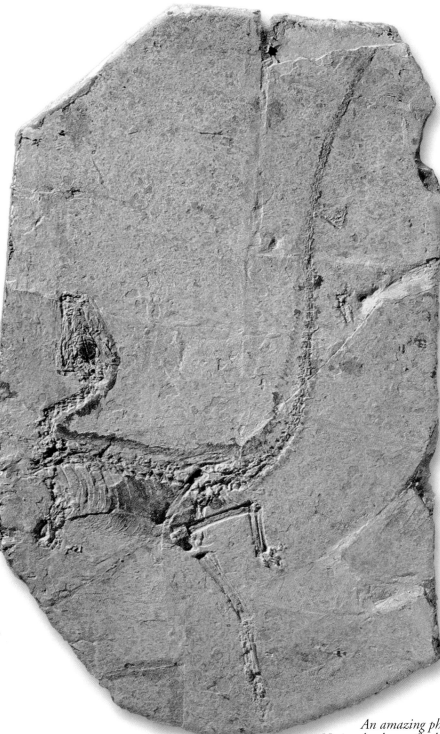

with feathers. But how could things as fragile as downy feathers be preserved for millions of years? In one word: volcano.

During the Early Cretaceous Period, 120 millions years ago, the ancient lakeside area that would become modern-day Liaoning was thriving with prehistoric life. But dangers were rumbling. The earth was changing. Volcanoes spewed lava and ash. Airborne ash sank to the bottom of the shallow lake, forming an ultra-fine lakebed. Animals that died and sank into the soft ash were preserved in amazing detail.

Lin Yin Fang's *Sinosauropteryx* fossil was wrapped in volcanic ash, and then layers of rock, until it was discovered in 1994. The gentle ash had covered and protected the fragile filaments, the hard center cores of the feathers that sprouted from its neck and hip. Some scientists who examined the fossil claimed the filaments were fossilized hairs. But Dr. Ji Qiang, director of the National Geological Museum of Beijing does not agree. "I knew these were feathers," he told *National Geographic* magazine, "because only mammals have hair and this was no mammal."

An amazing photo of Lin Yin Fang's Sinosauropteryx.
Notice the downy feather impressions surrounding the skeleton.

A Few Feathered Finds

Several fossils have been found that reveal impressions of what may have been dinosaur feathers. Even more exciting, new specimens are still being discovered. If you want to learn more about feathered dinosaur species, check out these well-known finds. Look in recently published dinosaur books or do an Internet search using the species' names below:

Archaeopteryx, Germany, 1861
Confuciusornis, China, 1995
Protarchaeopteryx, China, 1997
Caudipteryx, China, 1998
Microraptor, China, 2000

Three other *Sinosauropteryx* fossilized individuals eventually were found in the same prehistoric lakebed—and they have even more secrets to tell. One had two unhatched eggs fossilized inside its body near the pelvis. Finding the eggs near the pelvis convinced paleontologists that the female *Sinosauropteryx* had not simply swallowed the eggs whole, but instead was prepared to lay them. Another specimen had a prehistoric lizard preserved inside its stomach—the *Sinosauropteryx*'s last meal.

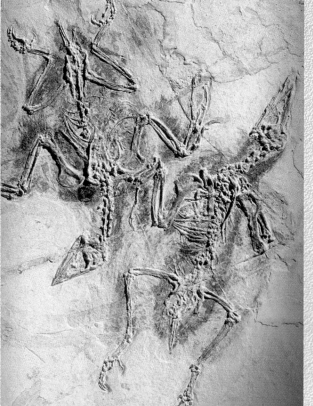

Left: Confuciusornis; *Middle:* Protarchaeopteryx; *Right:* Caudipteryx.

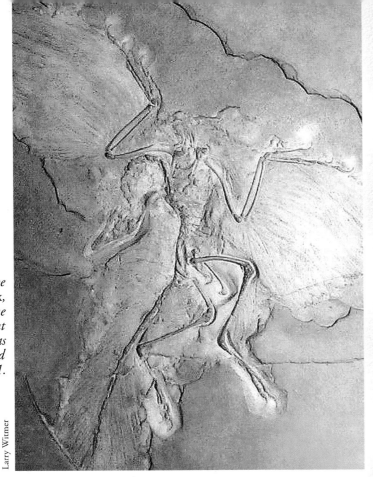

The Archaeopteryx, whose name means "ancient feather," was first discovered in 1861.

Larry Witmer

"[It] changes our perspective on what dinosaurs were," Dr. Norell said in an interview with the BBC News on March 6, 2002. "Instead of having scaly skin and looking like giant lizards, we now know they had feathers and may have looked like rather silly-looking, large birds."

Many more exciting fossils have been unearthed in the rich soils of Liaoning in China. But *Sinosauropteryx* was one of the first to prove that dinosaurs might still have cousins here on modern Earth—and that some of them are covered with feathers.

Who Is Dr. Mark Norell?

As a **curator** of paleontology at the American Museum of Natural History in New York City, 45-year-old Dr. Mark A. Norell is one of the most visible dinosaur scientists in the world. He spent most of his childhood in Southern California, a geographic region that is too young to have many dinosaur fossils to find. But he was still fascinated with prehistoric animals. He earned his master's degree in science from San Diego State University and was awarded his Ph.D. from Yale University in 1988.

One of Dr. Norell's special interests is finding an evolutionary link between small, meat-eating dinosaurs and modern-day birds. He is convinced that birds are dinosaurs' cousins, and he has spent a decade collecting information that could prove his theory. This determination has sent him all over the world and has given him the opportunity to appear in dinosaur specials on the Discovery Channel, other educational television outlets, and on videos. Dr. Norell has written several children's books about dinosaurs. He lives in New York City.

American Museum of Natural History

Dr. Mark Norell (right) with Dr. Ji Qiang

UNHATCHED SECRETS: TITANOSAUR EMBRYOS OF ARGENTINA

FOR MORE THAN 15 YEARS, Los Angeles paleontologist Dr. Luis Chiappe has believed some kinds of dinosaurs might be distant cousins of modern-day birds. When he joined a team of explorers in Argentina's Patagonian region in 1997, he was on the lookout for more paleo-evidence to prove that connection. Instead, he found something extraordinary: a longneck dinosaur nesting ground.

"We realized that we'd not only found hundreds of eggs in this nesting ground, but that many of these eggs contained fossilized **embryos**," Dr. Chiappe says. Even more amazing, on the bones of the tiny, unhatched giants, he found fossilized skin.

Dr. Chiappe and his fellow diggers were skeptical at first. How could such tiny bits of fragile skin survive millions of years? But as they discovered more and more of the scaly fossils, they were convinced. "It was skin that had been replaced by rock," Dr. Chiappe says, "with texture and shape identical to the skin that once covered the body of the dinosaur embryo."

Top: Fossil diggers remove dirt and rock to expose a titanosaur egg clutch. Bottom: View of Dr. Chiappe's nesting ground dig site in Argentina's Patagonian region.

Which once-thriving species left this nursery behind? "We know the embryos are titanosaur **sauropods**," Dr. Chiappe says. They were the first longneck dinosaur embryos ever discovered. "Titanosaurs were common in Late Cretaceous Argentina. We have found exquisite [embryo] skulls with many anatomical details that have confirmed it."

Dr. Chiappe also has a fix on when these eggs were laid. "We believe the embryos lived between 79 and 83 million years ago," he says.

Does this South American nesting site prove longneck dinosaurs lived in family groups? Not exactly, according to Dr. Chiappe. He believes that growing titanosaurs probably remained with their herd as it migrated. "But we don't believe youngsters remained near the nest," he says. Adult female titanosaurs gathered in groups every nesting season to lay their eggs near a prehistoric river. When the embryos hatched, they were only 12 to 15 inches long. Imagine! These tiny babies had mothers that were 40 to 50 feet long.

Young titanosaurs that wandered too far from the protection of larger herd members faced serious danger. "Large meat-eating dinosaurs also roamed the area," says Dr. Chiappe. "We found a complete skeleton of an abelisaur nearby."

Workers excavating a sauropod (longneck dinosaur) site in Argentina.

Hungry predators like abelisaurs (a *Tyrannosaurus-rex*-like dinosaur) weren't the only dangers tiny titanosaur hatchlings faced. Nature itself could be just as hazardous. "From time to time, the river would flood," Dr. Chiappe says, "and the flood would cover the nesting ground completely with water and mud, and the embryos would die inside the eggs." That is a sad ending for a dinosaur baby, but the soft mud covered the eggs and fossilized them. As a result, today's paleontologists have been able to find and study them.

Has the embryo skin revealed any surprising secrets? "We're still studying it," Dr. Chiappe says. Experts have used a sewing needle to gently remove rock from the patches of skin just to be sure the little embryos aren't damaged.

A baby titanosaur hatches. In the background, an abelisaur makes a meal of the hatchlings.

Abelisaur vs. Titanosaur

Dr. Luis Chiappe said Argentina's meat-eating (carnivorous) abelisaurs probably stalked the plant-eating (herbivorous) titanosaurs in the same region. But what did these two dinosaur types look like?

Titanosaurs were four-legged dinosaurs within the longneck sauropod group. They were some of the largest plant-eating dinosaurs ever to thunder across the earth—and they were the last of the sauropods to go extinct. Migrating in herds was one of their best defenses against predators. But they probably used their great weight and whip-like tails to repel meat-eaters that dared to challenge the herds. *Argentinasaurus* and *Andesaurus* are two species of titanosaurs that lived in what became South America.

Abelisaurs were big, bulky, two-legged meat-eaters with razor-sharp teeth, 3-D vision, and an exceptional sense of smell, like their faraway cousins, the tyrannosaurs. (Tyrannosaurs lived on the northern Cretaceous continent called Laurasia, which became modern-day North America.) Abelisaurs lived in the southern hemisphere on the continent called Gondwana, presently South America. *Abelisaurus* and *Carnotaurus* are two of the best-known species of abelisaurs.

Dr. Luis Chiappe at the Patagonian egg clutch site.

Who Is Dr. Luis Chiappe?

Dr. Luis Chiappe is on staff full-time at the Natural History Museum of Los Angeles County in California as an Associate Curator, but he's also a research associate at the American Museum of Natural History in New York City. He has studied the evolution of prehistoric birds for more than 15 years. He has also studied pterosaurs and crocodilians. Dr. Chiappe has searched for fossils in South America, China, the United States, and several other locales. He has had dozens of dinosaur articles published in magazines, such as *Nature* and *National Geographic*. His book, *The Tiniest Giants*, tells more about the titanosaurs, Patagonia, and being a paleontologist on a South American dig.

"When I found the first large piece of skin, the best we've found to date, I felt wonderful," Dr. Chiappe admits. "It's a very special feeling, knowing you are the first person to see something so unique, something no one has ever seen before."

More than 80 tiny dinosaurs were plucked from their nests on that dino dig. Their secrets are gradually being revealed, one egg at a time. Dr. Chiappe is determined to keep going back to Patagonia where many more titanosaur secrets are still waiting to be "hatched."

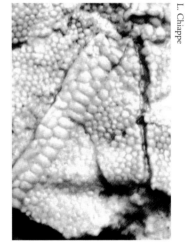

Left; A fossilized titanosaur embryo inside its shell. Right: Close-up photo of fossilized titanosaur embryo skin.

Leonardo, King of the Dinosaur Mummies

ON THE AFTERNOON OF JULY 27, 2000, more than a dozen professional and amateur bone diggers from the Judith River Dinosaur Institute in Malta, Montana, trudged over the rocky terrain. They were hot, dusty, and discouraged.

"It was very, very warm," says staff paleontologist Mark Thompson, in his thick Australian accent. "Ninety degrees or better. We were a little desperate. It was the last day of our field season, and we still hadn't found anything big to excavate in 2001."

So Nate Murphy, Phillips County Museum curator of paleontology and JRDI director, guzzled warm water from his metal canteen and headed in one direction with the guys. Mark Thompson and the women shuffled off in the opposite direction.

As the men made their last trek of the season, North Dakota fossil hunter Dan Stephenson headed toward a nearby sandstone ravine called a **coulee**. He'd passed it before, but Stephenson felt drawn to look at it again. He stared at a mound that was marked by an historic carving that read: *Leonard Webb + Geneva Jordan 1917.*

Stephenson found something astonishing sleeping beneath the sweethearts' names. "Leonardo," an amazing juvenile duckbill *Brachylophosaurus* fossil, had been discovered.

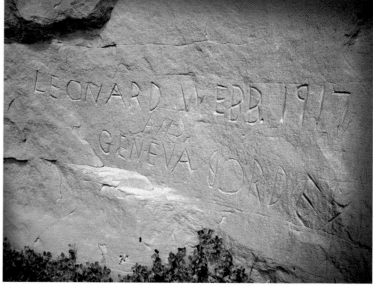

The landmark "sweetheart" stone that gave Leonardo his name.

Hadrosaurs, like Leonardo, sometimes migrated through fast-moving flood waters.

"[It was] the most beautiful dinosaur I've ever seen," says famed Colorado paleontologist Robert T. Bakker, who served as an advisor for Universal Studio's motion picture, *Jurassic Park*, and who examined the fossil a year later. More than 70 percent of its soft tissue had been fossilized along with its bones, making Leonardo the most complete mummified dinosaur that has ever been found.

Plenty of skin covers the 77-million-year-old, 23-foot-long fossil. Leonardo, a three- to four-year-old dinosaur, was not full-grown when he died. He is so well preserved that the scaly patterns of his skin are as easy to see as the nose on your face. Not only was this an amazing discovery in and of itself, but also beneath the skin, Murphy found muscle, tendons, footpads, internal organs, stomach contents, a spiny frill, a neck pouch like a camel's, and maybe even a tongue!

Before he died, Leonardo had lived under a very different "Big Sky."

"Montana looked like a Mississippi delta," Murphy says. "There were bayous and swamps, meandering rivers, and rushing deep creeks. There were cedar trees and magnolias and ferns. It was a very lush environment with lots of places for predators to hide."

Could a meat-eater like *Gorgosaurus* have caused Leonardo's death? Murphy admits it's possible, but because he hasn't found any life-threatening wounds on Leo's body, Murphy leans toward a different theory. "These were herding animals that migrated and traveled along the swelling waterways in groups," he says. "Animals that travel in groups sometimes drown while crossing fast-moving waters. Leonardo was buried very quickly without being eaten. That indicates a high-water event." In other words, Leonardo probably drowned during the rainy season.

Most paleontologists agree that Leonardo is the dinosaur find of a lifetime. Murphy agrees. "It's a huge responsibility," he admits. "I've taken careful notes and consulted every expert I can find. I owe it to Leonardo to do everything by the book. But there *isn't* a book. This is the first time a dinosaur mummy has ever been found and precisely documented."

At the Phillips County Museum in 2002, Nate Murphy unveils the greatest dinosaur mummy ever found: Leonardo. Leonardo's body was so well preserved that viewers can see fossilized skin, muscles, tendons, footpads, internal organs, stomach contents, a spiny frill on its neck, a neck pouch, and maybe a tongue.

Great Falls Tribune Photo by Stuart S. White

Who Is Nate Murphy?

Being the man in charge of a dinosaur like Leonardo tends to make people stand up and take notice. Now people want to know: Who is Nate Murphy?

Mr. Murphy is a third-generation dinosaur digger, born in 1957 in California. He cut his paleo-teeth in amazing company. Both his grandmother and his grandfather collected fossils for the American Museum of Natural History's famous paleontologist, Barnum Brown. Murphy found his first dinosaur when he was just a child—a child under the careful watch of Levi Sternberg, son of Charles H. Sternberg.

"It was in the Red Deer Valley of Alberta, Canada," Murphy remembers. "I was ten and the fossil was *Monoclonius*—it's called *Centrosarus* now. The [fossil-hunting] passion may have skipped a generation. My father never enjoyed fossils. But I was born to do this, and so was my son Matt. He's stepping into those same shoes."

Today Nate Murphy is the curator of paleontology at the Phillips County Museum in Malta, Montana, and he is also the head of the not-for-profit Judith River Dinosaur Institute. He spends almost every waking moment searching for or studying prehistoric dinosaurs. "I can't help it," he says. "It's in my blood."

Leonardo's Last Meal

Montana paleontologists were very excited to discover that Leonardo's stomach and intestines were among his many fossilized parts. Inside Leonardo's digestive organs, they found his last meal. So, what did Leo like to munch on?

"Mostly crushed-up fern and pinecone material," says Judith River Dinosaur Institute staff member Mark Thompson. "There were also some fibers that looked like they could be related to a magnolia-type flower."

Besides the plant material, Thompson also found tiny particles of pollen within Leonardo's stomach—dozens of different kinds of pollens, maybe as many as 40 or more. "That doesn't just tell us what he was eating," Thompson says. Plant life was so plentiful that Leonardo could even "get pollen from the water he drank." He continues, "There was one set of pollens in the front section of Leo's intestine and a different type altogether in the back. That probably means he was eating in different places on different days."

According to Thompson, Leonardo's main menu included "eight flowering plant pollens, fresh-water algae, and liverwort, all of which only live in tropical rainforests."

More studies will be done to help identify and understand the clues left in Leonardo's stomach.

Mummies like those found by the Sternbergs were collected and prepared, but no one took good notes to streamline the process for dinosaur hunters yet to come. Murphy was determined to do a better job. Why is Nate Murphy being so careful?

"For two reasons," he admits. "I want to help paleontologists who will find soft tissue specimens in the future. And I want to keep from going down in history as the guy who ruined the perfect dinosaur."

According to Murphy, Leonardo is a specimen that will change forever the way we look at dinosaurs. "Right now, studying him is like looking through frosted glass into a different world. I can't see it very clearly yet. But as we get better at this, as we collect more information, that frost will melt away. Leonardo will help us all see."

When Leonardo goes into paleontology history books, Nate Murphy will do his best to make sure that the story is as complete as Leo's fossilized body.

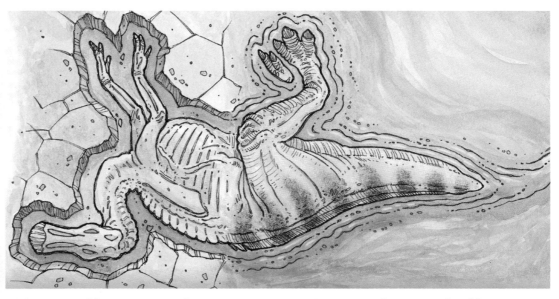

The process of dinosaur mummification occurs in stages. Over time, soft tissue is replaced by minerals, forming a cast of the animal. A layer of hard rock protects the cast. This hard rock layer had to be chipped away to "free" upside-down Leonardo from his grave.

WHY IS LEONARDO SO SPECIAL?

by Kenneth Carpenter, Ph.D.
Curator of Lower Vertebrate Paleontology & Chief Preparator
Denver Museum of Natural History

The specimen "Leonardo" is remarkable, not only because of the skin it has, but because the skeleton is barely crushed. Skeletons are usually flattened by the pressure of the overlying rock. Leonardo, the 3-D mummy, was protected by the sandstone in which it was found. Sand grains do not compact the way mud does. Mud loses 60 percent or more of its volume as the water is squeezed out to form mudstone.

I suspect that Leonardo mummified during a drought and got buried in a river channel sometime after the drought broke. We know from studies of animals in East Africa that large mammals seek refuge in water holes during droughts in order to keep from overheating. If the drought lasts long enough, these water holes dry up, leaving the animals (elephants, rhinos, hippos, etc.) to "fry" (so to speak) in the hot sun. We know from charcoal found in the [rock formations] where Leo was found that the forests occasionally got dry enough for forest fires, which means droughts did occur during Leo's time.

Studies of East African drought fatalities show that the carcasses can dry so hard that it takes a hacksaw to cut through the hide. Such tough skin takes a long time to soften once rain starts.

34

During a drought, a large animal, such as this cow, dies and dries up. The animal's hide becomes very hard, making fossilization of the skin and other soft tissue possible.

So it is easy to imagine that several days of heavy rain after the drought ended would not have caused Leo's hide to soften. The dried carcass could hold together until floodwaters brought in enough sand to bury Leo, probably in a matter of days.

Eventually, the ground water would soften the tissue, and bacteria would resume their work of decomposition. But bacteria need to rid themselves of waste. That waste would attach itself to dissolved calcium in the ground water and would form a layer of calcium carbonate around the tissue. That layer would become the protective **concretion**, or hard rock, paleontologists had to chip away to free Leonardo.

My experimental work shows that layers can form in a matter of weeks, and thus record or mold the surface or hide as an impression before it completely rots away. The rotting tissue is then filled in with minerals (a cast). So, what we really have of Leo is not an Egyptian-style mummy, but the record of the skin surface in a mold and cast.

Leonardo is without a doubt one of the best hadrosaur mummies ever found, and one that promises to provide much new information about this rare species.

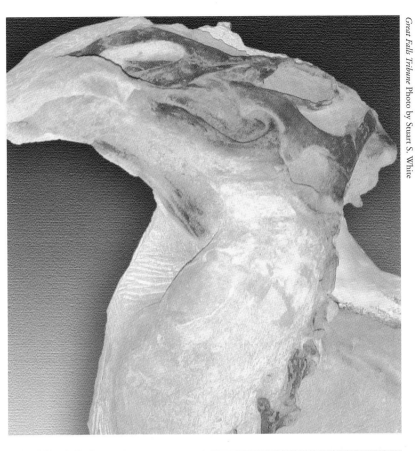

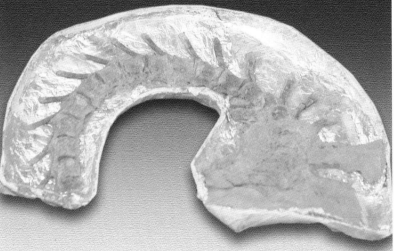

Above: A close-up of Leonardo's head and neck with fossilized skin and muscles.
Below: A close-up of Leonardo's tail section.

Great Falls Tribune Photo by Stuart S. White

Great Falls Tribune Photo by Stuart S. White

Bits and Pieces: More Amazing Dinosaur Mummy Discoveries

Barnum Brown

American Museum of Natural History

SPECIES: *Corythosaurus*

TIME PERIOD: Late Cretaceous

FOUND IN: Alberta, Canada

DATE FOUND: 1912

EXPERT IN CHARGE: Barnum Brown

EXPERT'S HEADQUARTERS:

American Museum of Natural History,
New York City

NOTES:

Famed dinosaur hunter Barnum Brown found a nearly complete *Corythosaurus* skeleton in Alberta, Canada, in 1912. To his delight, fossilized skin covered almost the entire left side of the dinosaur. The patterns were described as **polygonal** bumps, turning to oval bumps on the belly and pelvic regions. It is still on display at the American Museum of Natural History in New York City, New York.

You've read about six remarkable dinosaur fossil finds. Are these the only dinosaur mummy samples to be found? Not by a long shot. Other historic examples can be found in museums around the world. The story of mummified, fossilized soft tissue is far from complete. New chapters are being added almost every day. Take a look at this paleo-notebook to get a glimpse of more dinosaur mummy mysteries.

Dr. Jack
Horner

Bruce Selyem © Museum of the Rockies

SPECIES: *Tyrannosaurus rex*

TIME PERIOD: Cretaceous

FOUND IN: Montana

DATE FOUND: 1990

EXPERTS IN CHARGE:

Mary Higby Schwietzer, Dr. Jack Horner

EXPERTS' HEADQUARTERS:

Montana State University

NOTES:

While other paleontologists were studying fossilized skin and muscle soft tissue, Mary Higby Schwietzer and Dr. Jack Horner were studying the fossilized bone marrow of a nearly complete *T. rex*. These scientists found what seem to be red blood cells and other components of fossilized blood within the marrow. Studying those components will reveal many secrets about how *Tyrannosaurus rex* lived.

Derek E.G.
Briggs

SPECIES: *Pelecanimimus*

TIME PERIOD: Early Cretaceous

FOUND IN: Las Hoyas, Spain

DATE FOUND: 1994

EXPERT IN CHARGE:

Derek E. G. Briggs

EXPERT'S HEADQUARTERS:

Yale University

NOTES:

Near Las Hoyas, Spain, Derek Briggs discovered the mineralized skin, muscle, and other body parts of an ornithomimosaur, as well as an outline of its carcass. The fossil confirms that *Pelecanimimus* had a throat pouch and a soft crest on the back of its head.

Eva Koppelhus

Dr. Phil Currie

SPECIES: *Tyrannosaurus rex*

TIME PERIOD: Cretaceous

FOUND IN: Edmonton, Canada

DATE FOUND: 1995

EXPERT IN CHARGE: Dr. Phil Currie

EXPERT'S HEADQUARTERS:

Royal Tyrrell Museum, Drumheller,

Alberta, Canada

NOTES:

Twelve-year-old fossil hunter Tess Owen found a ten-centimeter impression in Edmonton, but she wasn't sure what it actually was. Famed Royal Tyrrell Museum paleontologist Dr. Phil Currie studied the fossil and discovered it was indeed dinosaur skin. But what made the discovery really exciting was the prospect that it *might* be a *Tyrannosaurus rex* skin impression. The skin was not found with any other fossil material, but Dr. Currie and other experts suspect that their *T. rex* hunch is correct.

Alexander Kellner

Dr. Alexander Kellner

SPECIES: *Santanaraptor*

TIME PERIOD: Middle Cretaceous

FOUND IN: Brazil

DATE FOUND: 1996

EXPERT IN CHARGE: Dr. Alexander Kellner

EXPERT'S HEADQUARTERS:

Federal University of Rio de Janeiro, Brazil

NOTES:

Very thin layers of mineralized skin and some muscle fibers were preserved on this dog-sized theropod skeleton. But paleontologists were especially interested in the preserved blood vessels and blood vessel channels within the fossilized bones. Studying the dinosaur's vascular system could help us understand more about how they lived.

UAF photo by Todd Paris

Dr. Roland Gangloff

American Museum of Natural History

Dr. Ji Qiang and Dr. Mark Norell

SPECIES: *Tetrapodosaurus*

TIME PERIOD: Mid-Jurassic/Late Cretaceous

FOUND IN: Colville River, North Slope, Alaska

DATE FOUND: 1998

EXPERTS IN CHARGE:

Dr. Rolland Gangloff & Professor Anne Pasch

EXPERTS' HEADQUARTERS:

University of Alaska Museum in Fairbanks, and University of Alaska in Anchorage

SPECIES: *Sinornithosaurus*

TIME PERIOD: Late Jurassic/Early Cretaceous

FOUND IN: Liaoning, China

DATE FOUND: 1999

EXPERTS IN CHARGE:

Dr. Mark Norell & Dr. Ji Qiang

EXPERTS' HEADQUARTERS:

American Museum of Natural History, New York City, and Chinese Academy of Geological Science, Beijing

UAF photo by Roland Gangloff

Theropod track impressions

NOTES:

These fossils are tracks that were left as dinosaurs migrated along what was once an Arctic coastal plain 90 to 110 million years ago. They include some four-toed tracks of ankylosaurs with pebbly textured skin impressions of the bottoms and sides of their feet. They also found unidentified oval-shaped tracks without toe impressions, which belong to some unidentified dinosaurs.

NOTES:

Trapped and fossilized between layers of limestone, a remarkable coyote-sized dinosaur was found covered with hair-like filaments or feather cores that were preserved along with muscles and other fine details.

Dr. David
Gillette

BLM/Grand Staircase-
Escalante National Monument

Dr. Alan
Titus

University of Chicago News Office

Dr. Paul
Sereno

SPECIES: *Hadrosaurs*

TIME PERIOD: Late Cretaceous

FOUND IN: Utah

DATE FOUND: 2001

EXPERTS IN CHARGE:

Dr. David Gillette & Dr. Alan Titus

EXPERTS' HEADQUARTERS:

Museum of Northern Arizona, Flagstaff,

and Escalante National Monument, Utah

NOTES:

Four hadrosaurs found in the Grand Staircase-Escalante National Monument have yielded dinosaur skin impressions—molds of the skin surface, but not the skin itself. Gillette and Titus hope to use the skin impressions to help study how hadrosaur skin patterns and textures changed as dinosaurs grew from hatchlings to babies to juveniles to adults to seniors.

SPECIES: *Tyrannosaur*

TIME PERIOD: Cretaceous

FOUND IN: South Dakota

DATE FOUND: 2001

EXPERT IN CHARGE: Dr. Paul Sereno

EXPERT'S HEADQUARTERS:

Field Museum of Natural History,

Chicago, Illinois

NOTES:

Paul Sereno hopes a small tyrannosaur he discovered and excavated in South Dakota will prove to be a mummified dinosaur—perhaps a *Tyrannosaurus rex* (it hasn't yet been confirmed). He believes it is mummified because of the 3-D look of the specimen's rib cage. If the dinosaur had been preserved before it began to decompose, its skin impressions—which would be the first confirmed and undisputed *T. rex* skin impressions—could be waiting beneath the sandstone.

Peter Larson

SPECIES: *Triceratops*

TIME PERIOD: Late Cretaceous

FOUND IN: Wyoming

DATE FOUND: 2002

EXPERT IN CHARGE: Peter Larson

EXPERT HEADQUARTERS:

Black Hills Institute, Hill City, South Dakota

DINOSAUR NICKNAME: "Lane"

NOTES:

One of the most complete *Triceratops* skeletons ever found, "Lane," also has good cross-sections of its skin preserved. At least four different types of skin are visible, including typical pebble-like patterns, large rosettes, and an unusual **rhombohedron**-shaped pattern that has never before been reported. More information will be available after the fossil is prepared in 2003.

Dr. Karen Chin

The Science of Coprolites: The Scoop on Poop

Thanks to their fossilized stomach contents, dinosaurs like *Brachylophosaurus* and *Sinosauropteryx* have shown us what goes into a prehistoric creature. But what comes out?

Dr. Karen Chin knows. When it comes to fossilized dinosaur droppings, Dr. Chin, professor and paleontology curator at the University of Colorado at Boulder, is the undisputed champion. It's her job to get the scoop on dinosaur poop, called **coprolites**.

Like human beings, a dinosaur's dinner determined its deposits. Paleontologists Wendy Sloboda and Tim Tokaryk found a huge, 17-inch, 2.5-quart coprolite in Saskatchewan, Canada. Dr. Chin believes it was "left behind" by a *Tyrannosaurus rex*. The coprolite's enormous size, plus the signs of shattered plant-eating dinosaur bone fragments fossilized inside the giant doo-doo deposit, helped prove that *T. rex* was the "poop-etrator" of the pile.

Herbivores left behind coprolites that contained plant matter: leaves, needles, seeds, and pollens. Both herivores and **carnivores** deposited poop with snails and dung beetles trapped inside. Their remains have been found in coprolites, too.

Chin studied under famed paleontologist Dr. Jack Horner at Montana State University. She received her doctorate at the University of California at Santa Barbara. Dr. Chin is respected by experts around the world—that's not bad for a girl who loves digging up dinosaur doo-doo.

A dinosaur coprolite.

MORE DINOSAUR DISCOVERIES— WAITING FOR YOU!

Books, videos, museums, web sites, and field trips can help you find more amazing fossil facts. These lists will give you a good place to start.

Royal Tyrrell Museum / Alberta Community Development.

Skeleton of a Tyrannosaurus rex

BOOKS

DINOSAUR GHOSTS: THE MYSTERY OF *COELOPHYSIS*
by Dr. J. Lynette Gillette, Dial Books for Young Readers, 1997.
ISBN: 0-80371-721-0
In prehistoric days, New Mexico's Ghost Ranch was home to the ferocious little meat-eater, *Coelophysis*. Dr. Gillette's fascinating book takes you to the *Coelophysis* bone beds. Found in 1947, hundreds of *Coelophysis* skeletons were stacked on top of each other. Dr. Gillette asks why they ended up like this, and he offers some answers about this swift, small dinosaur and its burial ground.

**DINOSAUR PARENTS, DINOSAUR YOUNG:
UNCOVERING THE MYSTERY OF DINOSAUR FAMILIES**
by Kathleen Weidner Zoehfeld, Clarion Books, 2001.
ISBN: 0-39591-338-1
For many years, scientists believed that all dinosaurs laid their eggs and then left the would-be hatchlings to fend for themselves, just as crocodiles and other lizard species do today. Then Dr. Jack Horner found a nesting ground of *Maiasaura* at Egg Mountain that proved some dinosaurs stayed around to care for their young. Weidner Zoehfeld's book explores this dig site, as well as other dinosaur-family discoveries. Many field photos are included.

DINOSAURS: THE BIGGEST, BADDEST, STRANGEST, FASTEST
by Howard Zimmerman and George Olshevsly, Atheneum, 2000.
ISBN: 0-68983-276-1
Although some reviews might say that this book is for children as young as four, don't let that scare you away. This oversized picture book is full of great dinosaur information—and awesome dinosaur illustrations from some of the best paleo-artists in the business.

DINOSAUR WORLDS: NEW DINOSAURS, NEW DISCOVERIES

by Don Lessem, Boyds Mills Press, 1996.
ISBN: 0-56397-597-1
"Dino Don" Lessem has been a dinosaur fan for more than a decade. In this book he offers readers a look at recent dinosaur discoveries, as well as ideas about how and where these dinosaurs lived. Dinosaur statistics and hundreds of illustrations add to the book's dinosaur value.

EXTREME DINOSAURS

by Luis Rey, Chronicle Books, 2001.
ISBN: 0-81183-086-1
Luis Rey is a dinosaur illustrator with a real flair. Mr. Rey searches for the newest, most accurate dinosaur theories and brings them to life through his illustrations. This picture book highlights Rey's talents, especially in his bird-like illustrations. And while not all paleontologists will agree with Rey's theories, most agree that his paintings are hard to resist.

FEATHERED DINOSAURS

by Christopher Sloan, National Geographic, 2000.
ISBN: 0-79227-219-6
This "Parents' Choice" award winner is a beautifully illustrated picture book about the theory of the bird/dinosaur relationship. Careful but interesting writing and exceptional illustrations make it a great book for dinosaur fans. The introduction by Canadian paleontologist, Dr. Phillip Currie, is a special treat for dinosaur lovers.

HOW TO DRAW DINOSAURS

by Michael LaPlaca, Troll, 2002.
ISBN: 0-81677-440-4
This updated version of Troll's *How to Draw Dinosaurs* is a great introduction to dinosaur drawing. The book includes several different species, including *Tyrannosaurus rex, Triceratops, Stegosaurus, Diplodocus,* and more.

JURASSIC PARK INSTITUTE DINOSAUR FIELD GUIDE

by Dr. Thomas R. Holtz and Dr. Michael Brett-Surman, Random House, 2001.
ISBN: 0-37581-293-8
This book offers 160 pages of useful dinosaur information written by two well-known and well-respected paleontologists. Illustrator Robert Walters provides dramatic dinosaur drawings. Added factoids about the *Jurassic Park* film dinosaurs make this a fun, unique field guide for dinosaurs.

JURASSIC PARK INSTITUTE DINOSAUR TRAVEL GUIDE

by Kelly Milner Halls, Random House, Summer, 2004.
Fossil fans all over the world will have a terrific travel guide to help them plan dinosaur adventures in the United States and Canada. The book details many exciting exhibits, lists a shopping directory for prehistoric goods, and packs loads of fun facts, interviews, and trivia in a handy state-by-state format.

NATIONAL GEOGRAPHIC DINOSAURS

by Paul M. Barrett, National Geographic, 2001.
ISBN: 0-79228-224-8
National Geographic Dinosaurs is a good overall book, featuring nearly 50 dinosaurs. Like most dinosaur fact books, it details the size, age, and type of each dinosaur, as well as its place of origin. Beautiful illustrations make this a great addition to your dinosaur book collection.

SEARCHING FOR VELOCIRAPTOR

by Dr. Mark Norell and Dr. Lowell Dingus, HarperCollins, 1996.
ISBN: 0-06025-894-2
Although this book is out of print, it's still one of the best dinosaur picture books ever written for kids. It paints a great picture of the real *Velociraptor,* rather than the oversized version shown in the recent films. Field photographs bring Dr. Norell's dig experience vividly to life. Try to find a copy at your library, at a used bookstore, or online. You'll find a great dinosaur treasure.

SECRETS FROM THE ROCKS: DINOSAUR HUNTING WITH ROY CHAPMAN ANDREWS

by Albert Marrin, Dutton Books, 2002.
ISBN: 0-52546-743-2
This photobiography of 1920s paleontologist Roy Chapman Andrews reveals much of what it was like to hunt for dinosaurs in the wilds of Mongolia, China. But it also explores Andrews's spirit of adventure and daring as he braved everything from sandstorms to sheep-eyeball soup.

THE DINOSAURS OF WATERHOUSE HAWKINS

by Barbara Kerley, Scholastic Trade, 2001.
ISBN: 0-43911-494-2
In the 1800s, Benjamin Waterhouse Hawkins built a collection of early dinosaur models in London, England, and later, in the United States. This picture book beautifully maps out Hawkins's passion for art and dinosaurs, thanks in part to Brian Selznick's Caldecott-Honor-winning illustrations.

VIDEOS/DVDS

CURSE OF *T. REX*
NOVA: WGBH Boston Video, 1997
ASIN: 6304462786
When the Black Hills Institute bone diggers found "Sue," one of the most complete *Tyrannosaurus rex* specimens ever excavated, they had no idea how much controversy they would stir up. This video follows the discovery of Sue and the legal battles over who was her rightful owner.

DINOSAUR! 4-TAPE SET
A&E Home Video, 1999
AAE-10100
Walter Cronkite narrates this video encyclopedia of prehistoric dinosaurs and the history of paleontology. It includes information about the "Bone Wars" of the 1870s, Dr. Jack Horner's "Egg Mountain" hadrosaur nursery, and theories of the bird/dinosaur relationship.

IN SEARCH OF HISTORY: SECRETS OF THE DINOSAUR HUNTERS
A&E Home Video, 2000
AAE-40469
This video chronicles the history of paleontology through its all-stars, including O.C. Marsh and Edward Drinker Cope and their "Bone War" fossil-finding competition. It also explores the controversy surrounding Sue the *T. rex* and Peter Larson's Black Hills Institute in South Dakota.

NATIONAL GEOGRAPHIC'S DINOSAUR GIANTS FOUND
National Geographic, 2000
ASIN: 0792290011
Look for three distinctive stories in this 94-minute video: Chicago paleontologist Paul Sereno's discovery of a new dinosaur species, a *National Geographic* photographer's search for dinosaur eggs, and a look at the controversy surrounding the *Tyrannosaurus rex* named "Sue."

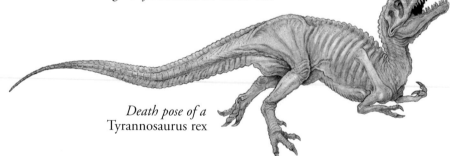

Death pose of a
Tyrannosaurus rex

NATIONAL GEOGRAPHIC: DINOSAUR HUNTERS
National Geographic, 1997
ASIN: 6304438133
Scientists from the American Museum of Natural History retrace the 1922 Mongolian paths of paleontology adventurer Roy Chapman Andrews. Some say that Andrews is the man who inspired the creation of the movie character "Indiana Jones." Archived photos and 3-D dinosaur animation make this a fun video to watch.

THE LOST DINOSAURS OF EGYPT
A&E Home Video, 2002
AAE-18384
In 1910, German scientist Ernst Stromer discovered dinosaurs in Egypt's "Valley of the Golden Mummies." Most of the fossils he collected were destroyed during World War II. Paleontologists returned to his legendary dig site for more than 50 years later. This video follows Josh Smith as he traces Stromer's path in search of Egypt's lost dinosaurs.

THE ULTIMATE GUIDE: *T. REX*
Discovery Home Video, 2000
ASIN: B00004REVN
This video offers a great look at the paleontological history of *Tyrannosaurus rex*, one of North America's more ferocious meat-eaters. Watch for models and excellent archive photographs.

WALKING WITH DINOSAURS
BBC Videos, 2000
ASIN: B00004ZEPU
Up-to-the-minute dinosaur science, wonderful computer animation, and well-written narration make this video a great family dinosaur experience.

WHEN DINOSAURS ROAMED AMERICA
Artisan Entertainment, 2001
ASIN: B00005MKL4
Featured on The Discovery Channel, this video explores dinosaurs that lived on what eventually became the North American continent. You'll see great interviews with famed paleontologists and lots of surprises, including 3-D animation of dinosaur anatomy that includes muscular structures. Some of the meat-eater sequences may be a too graphic for younger viewers.

Web Sites

http://www.dinosauria.com/
Dinosauria On-Line feels more like straight science than other dinosaur sites, because it includes hundreds of links to articles in science journals and newspapers.

http://www.dinosaurnews.org/
Designed for fossil fans of all ages, *Dinosaurnews Webzine* has news briefs, museum links, a dinosaur encyclopedia, and much more.

http://www.jpinstitute.com/index.jsp
Not just a commercial for Jurassic Park films and theme-parks, this is a great web site for dinosaur fans. Join a fossil club, dig into dinosaur travel stops, read the latest news flashes about dinosaurs new and old, and get to know your favorite dinosaur scientists.

http://dinosauricon.com
The Dinosauricon is another great dinosaur site with a dinosaur index, news, and article links. The most exciting feature of this website is its cross-section of dinosaur artists and their art samples.

http://www.bbc.co.uk/dinosaurs/
The *Walking With Dinosaurs* BBC web site offers more great dinosaur action, structured around the extremely popular British video, *Walking with Dinosaurs*.

http://www.enchantedlearning.com/subjects/dinosaurs/
Zoom Dinosaurs is a kids' dinosaur site, and its art leans toward the cartoonish. But there is a great cross-section of dinosaur information, all linked by related topics. Zoom is a good site for younger dinosaur fans.

Dig Site Destinations

Kids can participate in real-life dinosaur dig adventures at the following museums. Participation is limited, so be sure to write or call in advance for information about how much it will cost and how to reserve your spot. (Phone numbers and web site URLs are subject to change.)

Dinosaur Journey
Grand Junction, Colorado
www.dinodigs.org
Telephone: 888-488-DINO

Judith River Dinosaur Institute
Malta, Montana
www.montanadinodigs.com
Telephone: 406-654-2323

Paleo-World Dig-for-a-Day
Garfield County Museum
Jordan, Montana
www.paleo-world.com/DigForaDay.htm

Pioneer Trails Regional Museum Day Tours
Bowman, North Dakota
www.ptrm.org/page/daytour.html

Royal Tyrrell Museum Day Digs
Drumheller, Alberta, Canada
www.tyrrellmuseum.com/programs/
888-440-4240

U-DIG Fossils
Delta, Utah
www.threedee.com/u-dig/
Telephone: 435-864-3638

Wyoming Dinosaur Center
Thermopolis, Wyoming
www.wyodino.org
Telephone: 800-455-DINO

Mary Campbell

Landscape of Malta, Montana

BIBLIOGRAPHY

BOOKS

Carpenter, Kenneth.
Eggs, Nests and Baby Dinosaurs: A Look at Dinosaur Reproduction. Indianapolis, Indiana: Indiana University Press, 1999.

Chiappe, Luis M. and Lowell Dingus.
The Tinest Giants: Discovering Dinosaur Eggs. New York: Doubleday, 1999.

Chiappe, Luis M. and Lowell Dingus.
Walking on Eggs. New York: Scribner, 2001.

Currie, Phillip and Kevin Padian.
Encyclopedia of Dinosaurs. San Diego, California: Academic Press/Harcourt, 1997.

Norman, David.
The Illustrated Encyclopedia of Dinosaurs. New York: Crescent Books, 1988.

Paul, Gregory S.
The Scientific American Book of Dinosaurs. New York: St. Martin's Press, 2000.

Rogers, Katherine.
The Sternberg Fossil Hunters, A Dinosaur Dynasty. Missoula, Montana: Mountain Press Publishing Company, 1991.

Sternberg, Charles H.
The Life of a Fossil Hunter. Indianapolis, Indiana: Indiana University Press, 1990.

Sternberg, Charles H.
Hunting Dinosaurs in the Bad Lands of the Red Deer River. Alberta, Canada: NeWest Press, 1985.

ARTICLES AND WEBSITES

Brusatte, Steve. "Portrait of Cristiano Dal Sasso." PaleoZoic, 2000. Website: http://www.dinodata.net

Chiappe, Luis. "First Dinosaur Embryos Found with Skin," American Museum of Natural History. Website: http://www.amnh.org/exhibitions/expeditions/dinosaur/patagonia

"Feathered Dinosaurs of Liaoning, The." BBC News, December 26, 2000. http://news.bbc.co.uk/1/hi/sci/tech/1081677.stm

Guthier, Jacques and Gall, Lawrence F. "China's Feathered Dinosaurs." Peabody Museum. Website: http://www.peabody.yale.edu/exhibits/cfd

"Information on Tectonic Plates." United States Geological Service. Website: http://geology.er.usgs.gov/eastern/tectonic.html#plates

Norell, M.A. "Biographical Web Page." American Museum of Natural History. Website: http://research.amnh.org/vertpaleo/norell.html

Norell, M.A. "A New Feathered Specimen." American Museum of Natural History. Website: http://research.amnh.org/vertpaleo/dinobird.html

Qiang, J., P.J. Currie, M.A. Norell, and J. Shu-An. "Two feathered dinosaurs from northeastern China." *Nature.* June 25, 1998.

PERSONAL INTERVIEWS AND CORRESPONDENCE

Dr. R. Robert Bakker, Interviewed in October 2002. Director of the Jurassic Park Institute; affiliated with Colorado University at Boulder and with Tate Museum in Casper, Wyoming; author of *Raptor Red* and *Dinosaur Heresies*

Dr. Ken Carpenter, Interviewed in October 2002. Curator of Lower Vertebrate Paleontology and Chief Preparator, Department of Earth Sciences, Denver Museum of Natural History; author of *Eggs, Nests and Baby Dinosaurs* and *Dinosaur Systematics*

Dr. Luis Chiappe, Interviewed in Oct./Nov. 2002. Research Associate in the Departments of Ornithology and Vertebrate Paleontology at the American Museum of Natural History; Associate Curator and Department Chair of Vertebrate Paleontology at the Natural History Museum of Los Angeles County; author of *Walking on Eggs* and *The Tiniest Giants*

Dr. Karen Chin, Interviewed in January 2003. Curator of Paleontology, Colorado University Museum; Assistant Professor of Geological Sciences at Colorado University

Dr. Cristiano Dal Sasso, Interviewed in Oct./Nov. 2002. Laboratory of Paleontology, Museo Civico di Storia Naturale, Italy; author of *Italian Dinosaurs*

Dr. David Gillette, Interviewed in September 2002. Curator of Paleontology at Museum of Northern Arizona; former Utah State Paleontologist; author of *Seismosaurus* and *Dinosaur Tracks and Traces*

Dr. Thomas Holtz, Interviewed in October 2002. University of Maryland, College Park Lecturer; author of Jurassic Park Institute Field Guide

Peter Larson, Interviewed in Oct./Dec. 2002. Co-founder of the Black Hills Institute of Geological Research; author of *Rex Appeal*

Nate Murphy, Interviewed in Aug./Sept. 2002. Paleontology Curator at Phillips County Museum, Montana; Director of Judith River Dinosaur Institute

Dr. Dale Russell, Interviewed in October 2002. Curator of Paleontology, North Caroline Museum of Natural Sciences; Visiting Professor, North Carolina State University; author of *Tiny Perfect Dinosaur* series

Mark Thompson, Interviewed in Aug./Sept. 2002. Staff Paleontologist at Judith River Dinosaur Institute

Colleen Whitney, Interviewed in December 2002. University of California Museum of Paleontology at Berkeley, California

GLOSSARY

anole—five- to eight-inch-long tree-dwelling lizard with color-changing abilities. Common to the southeastern U.S. Nonpoisonous, it feeds on insects and spiders.

archaeologist—a scientist specializing in the collection and study of ancient human artifacts and the behaviors they represent.

carnivore—an animal that feeds predominantly on the flesh of other animals.

casting—a molded reverse copy of another object, such as a footprint pressed into damp sand.

concretion—a protective rock layer formed around a body or object. This layer or concretion is made of minerals different from the rock surrounding it.

conifer—evergreen trees or shrubs with cones or other similar seedpods or fruits.

coprolites—fossilized scat or "poop" of dinosaurs and other prehistoric animals.

coulee—a small ravine or dry streambed.

Cretaceous Period—the last section of the Mesozoic Era or "Day of the Dinosaur" in geologic time, theorized to have been 144 million to 65 million years ago.

curator—a professional in charge of a museum's exhibits and collections.

dinosaur—extinct, land-bound reptiles that lived during the Mesozoic Era.

embryo—a vertebrate animal prior to birth or hatching.

endocast—an exact copy of soft tissue inside a stiff or bony cavity, frequently the brain.

erosion—the act of being gradually worn away or diminished by degrees.

excavate—to expose or remove from encasement; in the case of dinosaurs, this encasement is rock, dirt, and stone.

extinct—no longer existing.

fossil—an impression or trace of an organism that is no longer living, but is preserved in rock.

hadrosaur—any members of a family of bipedal (two-legged), plant-eating dinosaurs called *Hadrosauridae*.

herbivore—plant-eating.

horny sheath—the stiff, bone-like outer covering of claws or horns of an animal.

Jurassic Period—the middle section of the Mesozoic Era in geologic time, theorized to have been 205 to 144 million years ago.

marine reptile—a water-bound prehistoric reptile that lived during the era of the Mesozoic's land-bound dinosaurs.

Mesozoic Era—The geologic "Age of Reptiles," theorized to have been 248 to 65 million years ago.

migratory—relating to or describing an animal species that wanders or migrates.

mosasaur—a family of large, extinct marine lizards of the Cretaceous Period.

organic—living or once-living.

organism—a living thing or being.

paleontology (paleontologist)—the study of prehistoric fossils; one who studies them.

polygonal—featuring a pattern of circular-like shapes.

pores—a tiny or minute opening through which matter can pass.

porous—having pores as a feature.

rhombohedron—a geometric shape similar to a raised, elongated diamond.

saponification—process by which fats are converted to a soap-like substance.

sauropod—dinosaur within the family of long-necked, small-headed, four-legged plant-eaters.

tectonic plates—moving layers of rock beneath the earth's crust.

theropod—dinosaurs within the family of two-legged meat-eaters.

Triassic Period—the section of the Mesozoic Era, theorized to have been 248 to 206 million years ago.

trilobite—a segmented prehistoric marine animal that regularly shed its skin.

ultraviolet light—short light waves, invisible to the human eye, that reflect radiation and energy.

INDEX